Theory of Change

A Practical Guide To Social Impact

By

Champion Muthle

Copyright © 2021 Champion Muthle

All rights reserved.

ISBN: 9798745308116

DEDICATION

To future Changemakers, young and old.
May you find happiness and success in your efforts.

CONTENTS

	Acknowledgments	i
1	Theory of Change	1
2	Objectives & Interventions	5
3	Entering Impact	10
4	Impediments To Impact	17
5	Change Management	22
6	Practical Impact	42
7	Good Pedagogy	55
8	Good Praxis	71
9	The Evolution of Impact	95
10	The Future of Impact	105

ACKNOWLEDGMENTS

I'd like to thank all the Changemakers, Charities, CEOs and Social Impact Strategists I've worked with over the years. Your efforts and ideas have not been lost on me.

1

THEORY OF CHANGE

Theory of Change can be simple. Social Impact can be immediate and profound. A Tribal dance around a flaming fire. A dropped pot by Ai Weiwei. A marching band in the middle of a protest. A Theater of the Oppressed performance in the middle of Brazil. Sean Penn in a riverboat. Skateboarders on a city street. A work by Banksy or Black Lives Matter. A church choir in the midst of suffering. A poem by Langston Hughes or

THEORY OF CHANGE

Tala Abu Rahmeh. Jacob Zuma singing Umshini Wam from the top of a parked car. And yes, even the echo of a nuclear siren in the midst of war.

The setting, spectrum and circumstances may change, but the idea remains the same: To impact; to create change. Theories of Change are as dynamic as the issues they confront. The dichotomies that exist between them are dynamic, as well: Desired outcome versus actual outcome. Intention versus obstacle. Individual freedom versus authority. Justice versus injustice. Liberty versus tyranny. Art versus institutions. Progress versus the status quo. Opportunity versus exclusion. And Good versus Evil.

In the midst of this chaos created by continued injustice, inequality, and corruption, it's no wonder that the power of a practical Theory of Change lies in its simplicity. When it comes to Theories of Change, minimalism, artistry and impact outweigh complexity, convolution and complication. Too many Theories of Change models and processes complicate issues and organizations more than they solve or resolve the problems they highlight. This is to be avoided at all costs. The simpler the Theory of Change (ToC), the more powerful the impact. The more complex the Theory of Change, the less effective the impact.

Some activists, organizations and organizers spend months, even years, designing and developing the perfect ToC. Others rush off into the world with the White Man's Burden in mind, trying to save and rescue everyone they can find. In the middle are the truly effective and powerful leaders, the ones who develop simple and repeatable frameworks for Social Impact; frameworks that can run silently in the background for decades without the need for risk, notoriety or reward. These are the leaders and ToCs we like; the ones that truly make a difference and make an impact that extends well beyond the money, time and support we give them.

Effective Social Impact is driven by these practical and pragmatic Changemakers. They wield a Sendakian power, a supernatural ability to change the world and our most negative ways without all the hardship and fuss. The artists and musicians of the Anti-Apartheid Movement. The protestors and power leaders of modern times. They proclaim things like: "I have a Dream."; "To be or not to be…"; and "Four score and seven years ago…". They speak and work with poetry, power and simplicity. They architect as much as they inspire. These practical

THEORY OF CHANGE

Changemakers and ToCs are the superheroes of our time, the guardians of past and present, and the guides to the future of social change. They are small in number, but big in impact. These superheroes of practical social impact are the focus of this book.

2

OBJECTIVES & INTERVENTIONS: SPEED, EFFICIENCY & SCALE

I grew up paintballing, quad-biking, and navigating the most dangerous stretches of African roads, so when it comes to rapid maneuvers I know a thing or two. That's how one should approach the world of social impact and social change: Speed, efficiency and scale. These also happen to be the three main elements of practical impact. Get in and get out. Either you can deliver the change that's needed or you can't. History is littered with the deeds and intentions of good men. The fallacy of incremental change has been pushed and professed by those in power for centuries. "Things take time," they say. "Rome wasn't built in a day." That may be true sometimes, but it doesn't have to be true all the time; and it certainly shouldn't change our potential for rapid impact.

Every single person—even a nobody like me—has the power to change the world. A good idea can come from anywhere in the world and from anyone. By that same token, developing a Theory of Change and unleashing it upon the world can take time, but it doesn't have to take much time. Objectives, outcomes, consistency and coherence are critically important, yes, but not if they erode or impede the natural course of action or intervention.

In its rawest form, Change is rugged, unfiltered and fast, not refined, formulaic and slow. People want to see change occur, not hear about it and wait for it to come around someday. Given the severity of the problems and challenges facing today's world, rapid evolution and reform is a must. We can no longer afford to sit and wait idly by for changes to take place, especially when we have the tools and technology at our disposal to see change introduced and implemented rapidly, even immediately.

If Change is possible, it should be possible every day of the week, not just Mondays and Tuesdays. That being said, it's important to understand the difference between true change and insight versus half baked arguments and overwrought ideologies. This is where the importance of the history, philosophy, and science of social impact comes into play.

As a very young man I had the pleasure of meeting Nelson Mandela. From that day forward I understood the power and importance of personal impact and principles. Like many liberation leaders, Mandela's strength and impact emanated from the power of his mind and demeanor and gravitated outwards towards the people who then reflected it back to him in the form of leadership.

As a Tribal leader, his power was immediate and profound. He embodied the very cause for which he stood. You could see the love, life, and sincerity of focus in his face. That's what made him, above all others, a great leader and the champion of the Anti-Apartheid struggle. This is a lesson I've carried with me throughout my career.

3

ENTERING IMPACT

If History and Philosophy are the one-two punch of social impact, Media & Entertainment are the KO. I realized the potential for Film and TV to change the world very early in my life. After my freshman year at American University, I decided to change my major from Politics to History, Philosophy & Film, with a focus on Cold War History, Social and Political Philosophy and

Screenwriting. When we see conventions being broken and change taking place on-screen, humans have a unique and rapid way of mimicking those changes in real life. That's real impact.

Given the size and scale of the industry, Hollywood can be the perfect vehicle for reaching the people and telling stories that inspire social change. The only person who felt the same way at that time was Jeff Skoll, Founder of Participant Media, so that's where I went to work right after graduation.

At Participant, impact was infused into the films we produced. We worked closely with nonprofits and community leaders so that audiences had something they could do, an action they could take, after seeing the film. The impact was tremendous. As a member of the Social

THEORY OF CHANGE

Impact and Advocacy Team, my job was to give people the tools they needed to make a difference on a given issue or cause they cared about, and to inspire them to expand their cause portfolio.

I worked on several films and documentaries, including: Food, Inc., The Informant!, Darfur Now, Fair Game, Good Night, And Good Luck., The Chicago 10, Casino Jack, American Gun, 3 ½ Minutes 10 Bullets, Angels In The Dust, Cane Toads, Charlie Wilson's War, Climate Of Change, Countdown To Zero, Furry Vengeance, Murderball, Oceans, Pressure Cooker, Standard Operating Procedure, The Cove, The Soloist, The Kite Runner, The Visitor, and Waiting For Superman.

During this time I helped design, develop and scale the Social Impact Index, a database of the most impactful

THEORY OF CHANGE

Social Change strategies, tactics, and campaigns across Media and Entertainment. That Index is now a staple of the Social Impact Sector.

After Participant, I went on to work at the Enough Project with John Prendergast at the Center for American Progress (CAP), The World Bank, and Advertising (McCann & Havas), before launching my own nonprofit, The Million Hoodies Movement for Justice (Million Hoodies), and several social impact-driven startups, including Mpwrd, Lavalytics and Zen Ventures, an impact venture studio for diverse founders, where I am today.

Each place I worked had their own unique angle and approach to social impact. I learned something new everywhere I went. The Enough Project combined hardcore policy recommendations with grass-tips, celebrity-style campaign strategy. It was highly effective at a time when young folks were passionate about joining their favorite celebrity in the jungle.

We worked tirelessly to end the deadly global trade in conflict minerals, violence against women in the Congo and a host of other critical foreign policy issues. John, JP as we call him, is the real deal. A genuine champion of Human Rights and Reform. He didn't just make movies about it, he put boots on the ground if and when the situation demanded. We all liked that about him; his passion was heartful and authentic.

I was lucky enough to contribute thoughts on the democratization of social impact for a chapter in his book, *The Enough Moment* (Crown, 2010), with Don

Cheadle. I was introduced to JP by the one and only Bonnie Abaunza, my former boss at Participant Media and a legendary Activist in her own right. Bonnie is the Founder of Artists for Amnesty International, one of the earliest nonprofit pipelines connecting Hollywood Celebrities to global social impact campaigns and organizations.

If Jeff, Bonnie and JP were my introduction to the world of social impact, the World Bank and the Advertising Industry were the perfect places to master my craft. At the World Bank I helped scale projects globally while making the Bank's Theory of Change as accessible to global audiences and stakeholders as possible.

At McCann and Havas I mastered the art of subtle persuasion, embedded impact and the high Art of

Advertising. Ironically, the campaigns and ideas I produced for brands and big businesses came to be more impactful and important than anything I had done before. Someone in the industry realized that potential for impact and decided to hire me. They were right, it worked.

By the time I launched my nonprofit, Million Hoodies, and my Creative Consultancy, Mpwrd, I had a ton of experience under my belt, several awards, and the confidence to, in the words of Gandhi, "Be the change I wished to see in the world." This was all I could ask for. My self-designed degree had served me better than expected, and now I was ready to hit another home run.

4

IMPEDIMENTS TO IMPACT

There's Theory of Change and then there's reality. The reality of the Nonprofit and Civil Rights Sectors is that there's a very small number of dollars that go to an even smaller group of highly manipulative and egotistical people with very narrow and often very antiquated mindsets and ideas about change.

For these people, it's not about progress or impact; it's about how many times they show up on TV, how many awards and accolades they can win, and how many young new players they can keep out of their way. For them, the longer the change process takes, the better; the longer people have to wait for change, the more money they make.

In all fairness, they've had to spend much of their time facing the music, too, kowtowing to corrupt politicians who are now in their pocket, so why would they change? To young Changemakers, however, this is profoundly pathetic, upsetting and counterproductive; it is, unfortunately, far too prevalent for any one of us to change on our own.

Just navigating this minefield alone can become a full-time job; and who has time for that? Life is short, and we can easily find ourselves getting tied up in the twisted and tangled wires of power instead of enjoying our lives and living happily. This phenomenon does, however, help us understand the real impediments to change: *Humans. Us.*

After your first year as a nonprofit leader, you begin to see the world for exactly what it is, and to understand exactly how difficult it could be to create lasting change. In short, your naïveté and previously unshattered vision of Utopia goes right out of the window! You find yourself having to enter and exit an endless stage and schedule that is not your own. It throws you off. It cuts you off. And yes, it cancels you. All the more reason for short, sweet and practical Strategies and Theories of Change. When the incumbents know they no longer have the goods, they turn their focus to destroying the new entrants.

THEORY OF CHANGE

The Media is the same way. You can see it in their shortsighted coverage of the issues. Many News Anchors and Journalists would agree. There is, in many ways, a revolving door of favoritism between producers (many of whom come from Hollywood), media networks and certain "celebrity" social leaders. But a good Social Entrepreneur never lets anything or anyone get in the way of them solving a problem or finding viable solutions.

This requires agility, adaptability, assertiveness and drive. One must become an expert swimmer in the unfriendliest of waters, and learn to navigate disaster with the skill of a seasoned Diplomat or a trained killer. Be warned, the choice is rarely yours to make.

5

Change Management

A Theory of Change is a methodology and process for defining the long-term goals of an organization and identifying the necessary preconditions needed to meet those goals. It outlines the causal linkages and pathways between desired and actual outcomes and models those outcomes before deciding on forms of intervention. It is a planning, participation, and evaluation process that companies, philanthropists, nonprofits, governments, and groups go through to promote social change.

The term Theory of Change was coined by Peter Drucker in his 1954 book, *The Practice of Management.* He defined it as a form of Management by objectives whereby organizations identify and follow high and low order goals in order to meet their objectives. As a theory, Theory of Change has its basis in Environmental and Organizational Psychology. It is a practice and process through which organizations change and manage the interventions needed to effect change. It also has a basis in Sociology and Political Science as a method of finding plausible, feasible, and testable solutions to social and political problems.

A Theory of Change starts with a macro "if-then" statement. What follows is known as an Outcomes

Pathway Diagram: A set of ideas placed diagrammatically in logical order or relationships to one another and connected with arrows that posit causality and precondition. It is a way of mapping long-term goals that are both "realistic and widely understood." The outcomes reached are usually stated in the form: "I'll know [X] outcome has been reached when I see [Y] indicator."

The process for developing a Theory of Change usually takes place in a workshop setting where a range of participants chart, plan, and propose possible objectives, outcomes, assumptions and indicators for their organizations to follow. The problem with traditional Theories of Change are the multiple layers of dependency, process and bureaucracy they create. There are also issues of linearity, cultural limitations and discontinuity.

The question naturally arises: Do Theories of Change serve to further frustrate or compliment strategic thinking and social impact efforts? This is a question we explore and revisit throughout this book as we unpack the history, structure, models, measurement, application, effectiveness, innovation, and growth of Theories of Change, and eventually propose new models that better meet the demands and realities of modern times.

Much has changed since the 1950s. The aftermath of World War II, the cultural and academic upheaval of the 60's and 70's, the economic and social changes of the 80's and 90's, and the political and technological changes of the 2000's. In recent years we've seen the War on Terror, the Obama Presidency, the Arab Spring, Occupy Wall

Street, the Tea Party Movement, the Movement for Black Lives, the Women's Movement, Code for America, and a myriad of other grassroots causes and popular movements. The consciousness and culture of the World has shifted in many ways that we haven't even begun to explore as it relates to social impact and Theories of Change.

Generally speaking, our impact models, processes, beliefs, and expectations related to social change have become stale and outdated. We've only just begun to incorporate the lessons of the recent past into things like policy, the workplace, academics and entertainment. When it comes to Global Culture, Pedagogy and Critical Theory, we are still in our infancy. In many parts of the world we're actually moving backwards, and in others, we continue to exclude the critical voices needed to create lasting change.

The question is one of reduction, integration, and improvement. In what ways can we reduce the complexities of current Theory of Change models, integrate the newest thinking, science and technology, and improve upon the most problematic thinking of the past? At the same time, how can we better account for global culture, critical theory, and pedagogy to help solve the issues of linearity, cultural limitation, and discontinuity? Let's take a look.

Linearity: Like Social Justice, Social Change rarely happens in a straight line. Like Evolution, Social Impact is not a straightforward linear process. Sometimes it happens in leaps and bounds. As Martin Luther King, Jr. and President Obama remind us, "The arc of the Moral

Universe is long, but it bends towards justice." As any good Screenwriter will tell you, linearity is dead; rarely does it serve as the structure of modern screenplays, character arcs or plots. Life is full of surprises, twists and turns, caveats and conundrums, swirls and sidebars, fake news and false positives. It requires us to shed our traditional beliefs in linear progress and chronological order. Past, Present, Future. Beginning, Middle, End.

As any nonprofit leader will tell you, the world tends to take one step forward and two steps back. That seems to be the way of mankind with all of our biases, insecurities, egos and ideologies. That's not to say that progress can never be linear, just that it rarely is. Change models that reify linear structures risk perpetuating outdated modes of thinking, supporting old school incrementalists and doing more harm than good.

THEORY OF CHANGE

Cultural Limitation: Traditional belief holds that change occurs through social and political structures, that can be modified, reformed and adapted to better fit the needs of the people. But as history shows us, these institutions rarely ever really change despite revolution, reform, and economic rejuvenation. Real change occurs in the form of culture, and culture is dynamic. It has a life of its own and can rarely be contained or pre-planned in the way that change models suggest.

The *Pluralism* and *Cultural Relativism* of Alain Leroy Locke clearly demonstrates this aspect of cultural dynamism, but his teachings have only just begun to make their way out of the classroom and into the real world. Cultural Relativism is the ability to understand a culture on its own terms and not to make judgments using the standards of one's own culture.

The goal of this is to promote understanding of cultural practices that are not typically part of one's own culture. Locke formulates his relativism in terms of the three principles of cultural equivalence, cultural reciprocity, and cultural convertibility.

Cultural equivalence is the idea that there are equivalent values and meanings across cultures; cultural reciprocity is the idea that values and meanings are inherently conditional and have correlates in other cultures and limited cultural convertibility, which is the idea that to a limited extent meanings and values can be understood across cultures by understanding how stringently those cultures associate their own value-forms with specific value-content.[1]

These three elements of cultural relativism help unpack the values that exist within communities, which can serve to either alleviate or complicate social outcomes, objectives and interventions.

Locke takes pluralism in all its form—religious, cultural, value, etc.—as a basic feature of the world. His primary focus then becomes one of understanding the multiplicity of ways in which people meet, and providing some normative guidance concerning how best to act when they do. Values organize, coordinate, mediate and direct experience. In so doing, they serve both a valuable epistemic as well as existential function.

---

[1] "Cultural Relativism." Lumen, 26 Apr. 2021, courses.lumenlearning.com/culturalanthropology/chapter/cultural-relativism/.

Values direct and guide our activity, but more than that they color the nature of our encounters with other persons, and frequently function as a source of conflict between individual persons and groups of human beings. The common mistake among valuers that leads to a "totalizing" of values as "absolutes" or "ultimates" is to forget that any given value encompasses only an aspect of reality and ought not to be treated as transcendent or reducible to that reality.[2]

Locke's presentation of his pluralist position proceeds as a response to three obstacles or barriers to pluralism: Absolutism, (counter) uniformitarianism, and arbitrary dogmatism. If individual valuers or value groups are able

---

[2] Carter, Jacoby Adeshei, "Alain LeRoy Locke", The Stanford Encyclopedia of Philosophy (Summer 2012 Edition), Edward N. Zalta (ed.), URL =
<https://plato.stanford.edu/archives/sum2012/entries/alain-locke/>.

to avoid these three pitfalls, then either may possibly develop a pluralistic value orientation.[3]

Discontinuity: As anyone will tell you, one of the biggest hurdles to achieving lasting change is discontinuity. Start, stop, start, stop, repeat. No matter how hard we try, it seems every organization falls victim to this challenge at one point or another. I can certainly attest to this problem.

The issue mostly lies in the difficulty of finding adequate funding and repeat commitment to the cause to support continuity and long-term growth. Many donors and philanthropists can be short sighted and spastic in their outlook; many Founders are inexperienced and ill-

---

[3] Guy, Talmadge C. "ALAIN LOCKE." Adult Learning Unleashed Consulting, ALU Consulting, 26 Apr. 2021, www.alu-c.com/alain-locke.

prepared for the cattle call that is the world of grant making and policy proposals.

One need only take a gander at Congress and the legislative process to see this broken, arbitrary and inconsistent system at work. They don't call it pork for nothing. Much of social impact and Corporate Social Responsibility (CSR) is a game of pay-to-play as well. It's difficult to know this as a newcomer, especially with all the rhetoric and PR around corporate responsibility and sustainability efforts.

Critical Theory: Theories of Change have their basis in Environmental and Organizational Psychology. And as we know, Psychology is an inexact science; what some may call a community of self-appointed quacks and backwards, "colorless" behaviorists. Much of the rigor and objectivity of the other sciences is, quite frankly, hard to find when it comes to Psychology. Environmental Psychology can be even more speculative and subject.

Thus, it can be argued that what Theory of Change offers in terms of convenience, it lacks in terms of critical theory. This goes hand-in-hand with what Dr. Cornel West calls the "American evasion of Philosophy." A problem [X] may very well benefit from a solution [Y] to create a favorable outcome [Z]. But rarely are psychologists, or even politicians for that matter, the ones best suited to classify and define these problems, solutions, and outcomes, especially in a cross-cultural, Third-to-First world context.

The legacies of Colonialism, the Cold War, and continued economic inequality leave much to be desired in the way of authentic progressive, practical, and pragmatic intersectional change. What's true for the First World is not necessarily true for the Third World, and vice versa. The legacy of the White Man's Burden must be dispelled, in part or in full, before true and lasting change can occur.

The opportunities, conditions, cultural contexts, and constraints surrounding social impact vary widely from one country to the next. They also differ globally and locally. Changemakers, especially those from the West, would do well to better prepare and inform themselves of such differences in advance of their changemaking efforts. Peircean Logic and Heideggerian Phenomenology have rarely been applied to social impact, but they definitely should be. That's just for starters.

THEORY OF CHANGE

Pedagogy: Global Education has evolved greatly since the 1950's. Pedagogy, the method and practice of teaching, especially as an academic subject or theoretical concept, has evolved greatly too. But those changes have yet to fully catch up with the world of Philanthropy and Social Impact, and vice versa.

This can be seen in the myriad of approaches to Education Reform and Public Policy in America, from Charter Schools to mandatory testing and No Child Left Behind. The lack of consensus and credibility around many of these proposals has a way of complicating an already complex and emotional issue, especially from the standpoint of educational laymen and outside investors. The topsy turvy power dynamics and institutional inequities that exist between Students and Teachers,

Teachers and Administrators, and Schools and the Public only serve to further complicate matters.

From the Bill & Melinda Gates Foundation to the Skoll Foundation, and the Chan Zuckerberg Initiative to The Emerson Collective, education reform initiatives seem to continually suffer from one or more of the abovementioned problems, and sometimes all three. Changemakers and Chanties alike would do well to revisit John Dewey, Michel Foucault, Orson Scott Card, and a number of other modern education theorists and writers before pushing new ideas and proposals onto the people.

Social Media: Perhaps the biggest and most obvious change affecting the world of Social Impact since the 1950's is Social Media. The majority of social impact practitioners are not Digital Natives and the majority of

THEORY OF CHANGE

Digital Natives are not Social Impact Practitioners. Thus, a divide exists between these two worlds. We could add Gamers and Computer Programmers to this list as well. We are only just beginning to unpack and understand the contribution and constraints of Social Media as it relates to social impact. But again, these lessons and studies tend to suffer from the same cultural hegemony and pedagogical differences from before.

As one of the first Social and Digital Strategists to work at the World Bank, I've seen the evolution, development and drawbacks of Social Media on the Social Impact and CSR Sectors firsthand. There is a lot of upside in this space, and a lot that we've yet to properly appreciate and understand, especially with regard to memes, movements, impact, and measurement.

THEORY OF CHANGE

After launching the Million Hoodies Movement for Justice in 2012—the only campaign in history, at the time, to surpass the Presidential Election in terms of Earned Media and Engagement—I watched in horror as the Media and Academia misconstrued, manipulated, and appropriated our message, cultural significance, and results into their own work and misguided criticisms of modern culture. This is a trend that continues to this day. It's significant because it obscures pedagogy and progress around social impact and social change, especially in terms of outcomes and measurement, which seems to be the point…to diminish its impact.

Take a look at the top social movements of the past two decades and you'll find that Million Hoodies is, by and large, missing from those lists, despite numerous impact reports, data, and mainstream media coverage of our results and effectiveness. Has History somehow magically changed or been erased? The movement and our subsequent campaigns all trended across social and mainstream media, even making their way into TEDx Talks, Harvard and Oxford Reports, but not into history books or Public Schools.

Why is this? And who decides? Could it be that when it comes to Social Media we are more interested in trolls, bullying and blacklisting than social impact and positive change?

6

Practical Impact

As we've seen, there are enduring creative, artistic, and existential elements to social impact that might be missed or unaccounted for by traditional Theory of Change models. In other words, there can be a big difference between Change Management and Practical Impact. An act of defiance may not be the same as an organization fighting for social justice, but its impact can be just as effective, if not more. A dropped pot by Ai Weiwei. A

Tribal dance around a flaming fire. There is an enduring cultural language and dynamism to these acts that transcends time and theory.

They hold a significance and power beyond incremental interventions and linear high and low order goals. They speak to a relationship and symmetry between moment and movement that might have previously been overlooked or antagonized by traditional theorists and politically motivated pundits.

What they may lack in process or testability they more than recoup in cultural cache, impact and effectiveness. They speak to the human spirit rather than the measuring mind; they issue a voice, flag and anthem that carries far beyond an individual bite, pixel, or social media post. They're inherently virtuous and therefore create a virtuous cycle of shareability, repeatability, and impact. They assimilate naturally into the cultural zeitgeist and appeal to laymen, artists, and professionals alike. They are both emblematic of the times and critical of them. They are both diplomatic and revolutionary. They harken back to the carrot and the stick, the Constitution and the Social Contract. They promote new pathways forward while resurrecting previously forgotten ones.

Rather than taking the form: "I'll know [X] when I see [Y]," they say, "When I see [Y], I'll know [X]." This is what we love about them. This is what we look to harness and replicate. They turn culture upside down and society, too.

I suppose you could say that my foray into social change and impact really began in High School with Model

United Nations. In 9th, 10th, and 11th grades I had the privilege of attending The Hague International Model United Nations (THIMUN) twice and helping launch the Johannesburg Model United Nations (JOMUN) at The American International School of Johannesburg (AISJ), my alma mater.

The American International School of Johannesburg (AISJ)

At a July 4th picnic celebrating American Independence Day in 1982, a group of interested Americans set up a table with posters advertising the opening of a new "American" school in Johannesburg. A few short months later, the American International School of Johannesburg opened its doors to its first students on September 6th. Founder Ed Norman, together with

THEORY OF CHANGE

American Embassy personnel and multinational businesses in South Africa saw the need for an American-style curriculum and international education for expatriates living in Johannesburg. Accredited by the State of Tennessee (USA), the school's first home was a residence in the northern suburb of Rivonia and the school opened its doors to 72 students.

By 1984 the school was bursting at the seams and the search for a larger facility was initiated. Two hundred and sixty acres were acquired from the Oppenheimer family. The only building on the campus was a crescent shaped stable for horses. The building was soon converted into 18 classrooms, and the school campus moved to its present location during the 1985-86 school year under the leadership of Director Dick Apple. As South Africa went through the dark days of apartheid, the school's population dwindled through the late 80's and early 90's.

But 1994 ushered in a new era of democracy for South Africa and since then the country has seen an influx of global interest and investment. Director Everett Gould saw the opportunities of a new free South Africa and how that would impact the growth of the school, which in 1995 had 395 students. He served as director from 1992-1998 and during that period AISJ continued development of its campus beyond the horse stables building. The High School wing was added, as was a new swimming pool, cafeteria, library, gym, Fine Arts Center and boarding houses. The Elementary School wing was added in 1995-96. By the year 2000, the student population stood at 530 students.

The Hague International Model United Nations

(THIMUN)

The THIMUN conference is a five-day simulation of the United Nations for secondary school students, which takes place at the end of January each year in the World Forum Convention Center in The Hague. THIMUN now attracts over 3,200 students and teachers from around 200 schools located in countries as far apart as Norway, Australia, China and Ecuador. The students themselves originate from more than 100 different countries.

The Hague, City of Peace and Justice, is closely associated with the United Nations. It is the seat of the International Court of Justice (ICJ), the International Criminal Court (ICC), the International Criminal Tribunal for the Former Yugoslavia and the

Organization for the Prohibition of Chemical Weapons (OPCW). In addition, The Hague is the seat of the Dutch government and many national and European Union institutions.

It is also the residence of the Dutch Royal Family, which has been very supportive over the years. Her Majesty Queen Beatrix was guest of honor at the XV and the XX Anniversary Sessions and Crown Prince Willem Alexander, a former delegate himself, formally opened the XXV Anniversary Session in 1993 and the Annual Session in 2000. King Willem Alexander attended the 50th Anniversary Session of THIMUN The Hague and formally opened it.

Although the majority of participating schools are English-language-medium schools, a large number of participants attend schools where languages other than English are the medium of instruction. For such students, THIMUN offers an excellent opportunity to expand, develop and put into practice English language skills, on an informal as well as a formal level. All the associated activities such as preparing resolutions, lobbying and debating are carried out in English and a high standard is demanded in the formulation of ideas, whether in writing resolutions or in arguing and debating with fellow students.

THIMUN is organized by the THIMUN Foundation, headquartered in The Hague, in the Netherlands. The mission of the THIMUN Foundation is to promote and foster collaborative solution-oriented discussion to important global issues by instilling a life-long passion in youth to take an engaging role in the future and become more responsible global citizens. Attendants of THIMUN conferences seek, through discussion, to negotiate and debate solutions to the various problems of the world: e.g. questions of human rights, protection of the environment, economic development, disarmament, the problems of youth and of refugees, as well as the more critical issues of war and peace.

The young delegates, in seeking solutions to these problems, can learn to break away from narrow, national self-interest and develop true international cooperation. The research and preparation required, the adoption of views and attitudes other than their own, the involvement and interaction with so many other young people from around the world, all combine to give the young people a deep insight into the world's problems, to make them aware of the causes of conflict between nations and to lead them to a better understanding of interests and motivation of others.

Thus, the THIMUN Foundation, through its conferences and educational programs, attempts to fulfill the aims and goals set by the founders of the United Nations in the Preamble to the Charter of the United Nations: "…to practice tolerance and live together in peace with one another as good neighbours."

Model UN is great as both a training model, a teaching model, and an impact model. It builds maturity in young people, giving them agency, independence, and power at a critical point in their development. It also reinforces morals, ethics, and a global worldview to match the reality of our world. From a process standpoint, it teaches students Parliamentary Procedure, Resolution writing, and public speaking. It also reinforces consensus building, cross-cultural communication, diplomacy, and foreign policy.

Students gain insight into what it takes and what it's like to work at the UN while the UN gets a collection of the best policy proposals and resolutions from some the brightest young minds in the world. It's a win-win situation for everyone, and creates a virtuous cycle of interventions and high and low order goals. The structure of the program reinforces the vision, mission, and goals of the organization in a way that compliments and perfectly supports the impact model. The outcomes proposed are not only plausible, feasible and testable, but realistic and widely understood.

In addition to all this, Model UN gives students a chance

to travel, see the world and learn from different cultures. It builds a confidence and maturity that carries students confidently into college and the real world with the tools they need to be confident, critical and successful. Not to mention it's one hell of a party.

7

GOOD PEDAGOGY

These were the highlights of my High School years. Model UN served as the perfect complement to the International Baccalaureate Program (IB) at AISJ.

International Baccalaureate (IB)

The IB Program offers four high quality, challenging educational programmes to students aged 3 to 19. The program focuses on fostering critical thinking and building problem-solving skills, while encouraging diversity, international mindedness, curiosity, and a healthy appetite for learning and excellence.

An IB education provides students distinct advantages as they enter a world where asking the right questions is as important as discovering answers. For over 50 years, the global IB community of world class educators and coordinators has engaged with more than 1.4 million students in over 5,300 schools across 158 countries.

For me, what was great about the IB Program is that it stressed History, Writing, Comprehension and a spectacular little course called Theory of Knowledge (ToK). Funny enough, I never took ToK, but the idea behind such a course stuck with me, and the writing and comprehension skills I gained from IB have continued to serve me well to this day.

THEORY OF CHANGE

Let's just get this out of the way early: The International Baccalaureate Program beats Advanced Placement (AP) hands down. It's the perfect combination of macro and micro, theory and praxis. Its emphasis on the social sciences, freedom of thought and expression, and rigorous critical inquiry distinguishes it from other education programs and pedagogical frameworks out there.

Students come away with a comprehensive and complete picture of the world and their place in it. It connects past, present and future in a way that emphasizes critical thinking, deep comprehension, literary style, math and science, and purpose.

Theory of Knowledge (ToK) serves as the perfect compliment to a rigorous course load. Like Philosophy, it challenges students to question and account for how they know what they know, why they know it, and ponder upon what they don't know. As far as epistemological processes go, it forms the perfect compliment to Theory of Change models.

In terms of outcomes and pathways, there is something left to be desired when it comes to the rigorous examinations, make or break scoring system, and somewhat inconsistent course schedule. But taken as a whole, it is, perhaps, the closest thing to Dewey's vision of educational excellence on the market.

There's also something to be said about the quality of the teachers the program recruits from around the world. They really know their stuff. They jumpstart the student's education in a way that keeps them interested in the material and wanting to be successful lifetime learners.

Later on, in college at American University in Washington, DC, I joined the nation's first Student Think Tank, the Roosevelt Institute, and helped launch a Chapter at AU.

The American University (AU)

The American University was established in the District of Columbia by an Act of Congress on December 5, 1892, primarily due to the efforts of Methodist bishop John Fletcher Hurst, who aimed to create an institution that could train future public servants. Hurst also chose the site of the university, which at the time was the rural periphery of the District.

THEORY OF CHANGE

After more than three decades devoted principally to securing financial support, the university was officially dedicated on May 15, 1914, with its first instructions beginning October of that year, when 28 students were enrolled, 19 of whom were graduates and the remainder special students not candidates for a degree. The First Commencement, at which no degrees were awarded, was held on June 2, 1915.

The Second Annual Commencement was held the following year and saw the awarding of the first degrees: one master's degree and two doctor's degrees. AU admitted both women and African Americans, which was uncommon in higher education at the time. Among its first 28 students were five women, while an African American doctoral student was admitted in 1915. President John F. Kennedy delivered the

THEORY OF CHANGE

Commencement Address at American University on June 10, 1963.

In 1997, American University of Sharjah, the only coeducational, liberal arts university in the United Arab Emirates, signed a two-year contract with AU to provide academic management, a contract which has since been extended multiple times. A team of senior AU administrators relocated to Sharjah to assist in the establishment of the university and guide it through the Middle States Association of Colleges and Schools accreditation process.

American University's alumni, faculty, and staff have included two Pulitzer Prize winners, two Nobel Prize winners, one United States Senator, 25 United States Representatives, 18 Ambassadors of the United States, and several foreign heads of state. American University is one of the top five feeder schools to the U.S. Foreign Service, Congressional staff, and other governmental agencies.

The Roosevelt Institute & Campus Network

The Roosevelt Institute is a think tank, a student network, and the nonprofit partner to the Franklin D. Roosevelt Presidential Library and Museum that, together, are learning from the past and working to redefine our collective future. Focusing on corporate and public power, labor and wages, and the economics of race and gender inequality, the Roosevelt Institute unifies experts, invests in young leaders, and advances progressive policies that bring the legacy of Franklin and Eleanor into the 21st century.

THEORY OF CHANGE

Roosevelt takes on today's greatest challenges by advancing bold, cutting-edge research and policy ideas. It believes that the future of the American economy and democracy depends on a new way of thinking about markets and government. Roosevelt finds that too few people hold too much economic and political power today, and knows that a stronger society is possible if we rectify this imbalance between private actors and the public.

With a commitment to transforming corporations, restructuring markets, reviving democratic institutions, and reimagining the role of government, their work moves our nation toward a more resilient, equitable, and green future.

THEORY OF CHANGE

In 2019, Vox called on progressives to "listen to the Roosevelt Institute: Our policy problems are downstream from our power problems, and so the best way to fix policy is to start by fixing power." The Roosevelt Network trains, develops, and supports emerging progressive policymakers, researchers, and advocates on campuses and in cities across the US, focusing on communities historically denied political power.

Found on campuses and in cities across nearly 40 states, the Roosevelt Network is built on the principle that changing who writes the rules can help fulfill the ideals of American democracy and build true public power. The network supports student-led, scalable policy campaigns that fight for the equitable provision, distribution, and accessibility of public goods at the campus, local, and state levels. In addition to its student-led activities, the program leverages the power of its alumni network—which includes public officials, lawyers, teachers, nonprofit executives, and researchers—to expand opportunities for the next generation of policy leaders.

A program of the Roosevelt Institute, the Roosevelt Network operates alongside leading economists and political scientists to bring the ideals of Franklin and Eleanor Roosevelt into the 21st century. The Network envisions a world where the ideals of democracy are fulfilled in America so there is true public power through our government. The Roosevelt Network changes who writes the rules by training, developing, and supporting emerging progressive policymakers, researchers, and advocates across the US, focusing on communities historically denied political power.

THEORY OF CHANGE

As a program of the Roosevelt Institute, the Roosevelt Network operates alongside leading economists and political scientists in Roosevelt's think tank to bring the ideals of Franklin and Eleanor Roosevelt into the 21st century. The Institute is also the nonprofit partner to the FDR Presidential Library.

The Roosevelt Network is run by a team of full-time staff members based in New York. National staff members are not students; it is their full-time job to support the work of students across the network. The network organizes its chapters into five regions: Northeast, Mid-Atlantic, South, Midwest, West. Each region has a three-person team that works to organize student chapters.

Regional Coordinators: Oversee the region as a whole

and set a vision or direction. They take the lead on region-wide events, actions, or policy work.

Chapter Organizers: Work directly with established chapters to set goals, establish structures, host events, and more.

New Chapter Coordinators: Research and recruit people on target campuses in each region, and help folks build chapters on their campuses or in their cities.

The network has seven policy coordinators who lead in an issue area. They support student-led projects in this area across the whole country. The issue areas include: Education, Economy, Human Rights, Democratic Access, Energy & Environment, Healthcare, and the Financialization of Higher Education. The network also has two other positions on its leadership team.

Communications Coordinators: The communications coordinators focus on chapter-level press and promotion, as well as chapter-level digital strategy. They work with chapters and projects across all regions.

Community College Organizers: Two student organizers focus on building relationships with community college faculty and administration across the country. Their goal is to eventually seed chapters at these institutions.

As far as social change models and impact structures go, The Roosevelt Institute and Campus Network is one of the best there is. It connects students to the policy-making process and helps them present those policy proposals to members of Congress, a critically important task. A college campus-based chapter model supported by a national organization is the perfect structure for dynamic and sustainable action to take place.

Students are able to select their favorite issue areas and receive funding and support for activities and tasks on an ad-hoc basis. There's also a regular call for papers, quarterly reports speaking opportunities, publishing opportunities, chapter meetings, and a national meetup once or twice a year at the Roosevelt Estate in upstate New York.

Roosevelt started out small and nimble and continues to grow larger over time. The AU chapter was one of the first to introduce a focus on Native American Rights and continues to have a heavy emphasis on National Security, Environmental Sustainability and Foreign Policy. By the time I graduated in 2008, we were one of the largest and most active chapters in the network.

These five programs, AISJ, MUN, IB, The American University, and the Roosevelt Institute formed the basis of my foundation in public service, social strategy and social impact, and serve as the perfect examples of effective and long lasting social change programs and practical Theory of Change models, especially in terms of pedagogy.

8

GOOD PRAXIS

If AISJ, MUN, IB, AU, and Roosevelt represent the best of the best in terms of clarity of mission, robustness, and effectiveness of Theory of Change, our next list of organizations stand out for the strength of their models, their consistency, accuracy and modern approach. When it comes to practicality of impact, these traits are of utmost importance.

THEORY OF CHANGE

The Boys & Girls Clubs of America

Denzel Washington once said "Luck is when opportunity meets Preparation." That's exactly what the Boys and Girls Clubs of America provide: Opportunity and Preparation. The mission of the Boys and Girls Clubs is to enable all young people, especially those who need it most, to reach their full potential as productive, caring, responsible citizens.

Their vision is to provide a world-class Club Experience that assures success is within reach of every young person who enters their doors, with all members on track to graduate from high school with a plan for the future, demonstrating good character and citizenship, and living a healthy lifestyle. They believe every kid has what it takes.

THEORY OF CHANGE

The mission and core beliefs of Boys & Girls Clubs fuels their commitment to promoting safe, positive and inclusive environments for all. Boys & Girls Clubs of America supports all youth and teens—of every race, ethnicity, gender, gender expression, sexual orientation, ability, socio-economic status, and religion—in reaching their full potential.

The Boys & Girls Clubs of America had its beginnings in 1860 with three women in Hartford, Connecticut: Mary Goodwin, Alice Goodwin, and Elizabeth Hammersley. Believing that boys who roamed the streets should have a positive alternative, they organized the first Club. With character development as the cornerstone of the experience, the Club focused on capturing boys interests, improving their behavior and increasing their personal expectations and goals. A cause was born. In 1906, several Boys Clubs decided to affiliate.

The Federated Boys Clubs in Boston was formed with 53 member organizations—this marked the start of a nationwide Movement and a national organization. In 1931, the Boys Club Federation of America became Boys Clubs of America. In 1956, Boys Clubs of America celebrated its 50th anniversary and received a U.S. Congressional Charter.

To recognize the fact that girls are a part of their cause, the national organization's name was changed to Boys & Girls Clubs of America in 1990. Accordingly, Congress amended and renewed their charter. 2006 marked the Centennial year of Boys & Girls Clubs of America, as they celebrated 100 years of providing hope and opportunity to young people across the country.

Their network of after-school programs and support systems offer students a safe, healthy and supportive environment in which to grow and thrive. It also serves the needs of parents, communities and teachers who might otherwise struggle to protect and provide for young folks in the after-school hours. Not only has the Boys & Girls Clubs remained consistent, they've grown and matured in ways that solidify them as one of the best social impact programs in the country and a solid Theory of Change model to emulate and follow.

The Southern Poverty Law Center

There are some organizations that understand the necessity and importance of a precise and powerful legal approach. They see the writing on the wall well before others and project their power into the future in legal battle after legal battle in an effort to protect victims and their loved ones. The Southern Poverty Law Center (SPLC) is one such organization.

The SPLC is a catalyst for racial justice in the South and beyond, working in partnership with communities to dismantle white supremacy, strengthen intersectional movements, and advance the human rights of all people.

Civil Rights lawyers Morris Dees and Joseph Levin Jr. founded the SPLC in 1971 to ensure that the promise of the Civil Rights Movement became a reality for all. Since then, they've won numerous landmark legal victories on behalf of the exploited, the powerless and the forgotten. Their lawsuits have toppled institutional racism and stamped out remnants of Jim Crow segregation; destroyed some of the nation's most violent white supremacist groups; and protected the civil rights of children, women, the disabled, immigrants and migrant workers, the LGBTQ community, prisoners, and many others who faced discrimination, abuse or exploitation.

The SPLC Intelligence Project is internationally known for tracking and exposing the activities of hate groups and other domestic extremists. The SPLC Learning for Justice Initiative provides free resources to caregivers and educators—teachers, administrators, counselors and other practitioners—who work with children from kindergarten through high school. Educators use the materials to supplement the curriculum, to inform their practices, and to create civil and inclusive school communities where children and youth are respected, valued and welcome participants.

The SPLC also built and maintains the Civil Rights Memorial and its interpretive center, the Civil Rights Memorial Center, in Montgomery, Alabama, the birthplace of the modern Civil Rights Movement. They're based in Montgomery and have offices in Atlanta, Tallahassee, Miami, New Orleans, and Jackson, Miss. The SPLC has worked tirelessly and diligently to uncover, dismantle, and reduce some of the worst crimes, criminals, systemic issues and social injustices of our time.

Their Theory of Change model is precise, practical and effective. Not only does the SPLC map the problem perfectly, they've introduced new platforms and programs to help meet the needs of the rapidly evolving landscape. Their founders, leadership and volunteers are perhaps the closest thing to superheroes the world has, standing tall in the face of violence, death threats, massive upheaval, political opponents, and profound ugliness and injustice.

They make use of the Constitution and the courts in a way that is both progressive, patriotic and prescriptive. In so doing, they help protect the future not just for their clients and stakeholders, but for all of us. This is true impact. This is true change.

Freedom of the Press Foundation

There's no substitute for good journalism and investigative reporting. At a time when the safety and security of journalists has come under repeated attack, a handful of organizations have come together to help protect the freedom of the press and secure the future of that freedom. One such organization is Freedom of the Press Foundation.

Freedom of the Press Foundation (FPF) is a 501(c)3 nonprofit organization that protects, defends, and empowers public-interest journalism in the 21st century. The organization works to preserve and strengthen First and Fourth Amendment rights guaranteed to the press through a variety of avenues, including the development of encryption tools, documentation of attacks on the press, training newsrooms on digital security practices, and advocating for the public's right to know.

Freedom of the Press Foundation is built on the recognition that this kind of transparency journalism—

from publishing the Pentagon Papers and exposing Watergate, to uncovering the NSA's warrantless wiretapping program and CIA secret prisons—doesn't just happen. It requires dogged work by journalists, and often, the courage of whistleblowers and others who work to ensure that the public actually learns what it has a right to know.

The foundation's SecureDrop platform aims to allow confidential and secure communication between journalists and their sources, and has been adopted by more than 65 news organizations globally. It also manages the U.S. Press Freedom Tracker, a database of press freedom violations in the United States. FPF has also built a variety of experimental technology projects that aim to protect journalists or promote transparency.

In 2017, they helped release an Android app called Haven, which can use the sensors on anyone's smartphone to act as a security system for their surroundings. The project is open source and does not send any information to the cloud. They also built a Twitter bot called FOIA Feed which automatically collects stories that rely on the Freedom of Information Act from over a dozen different news outlets. Additionally, they built a tool that can archive at-risk news outlets which are in danger of being blocked or deleted from the web.

FPF engages in public and legal advocacy around critical press freedom issues, including excessive government secrecy, the protection of whistleblowers, the surveillance of journalists, the Freedom of Information Act, and reporter's privilege.

THEORY OF CHANGE

Nonprofit media, independent transparency organizations, and open-source security tools are increasingly a critical component of the journalism landscape. FPF aims to broaden the financial base of these types of projects by crowd-sourcing funding and making it easy for people to support the best journalism from an array of organizations all in one place.

The vision of FPF is to protect and promote the basic human right of freedom of the press, both in the United States, and abroad, in a world where surveillance, censorship, and manipulation are becoming more sophisticated and more pervasive. They understand that Public interest journalism—"the kind of journalism that holds power accountable and defends human rights"—is under threat everywhere. Their goal is to ensure that all news organizations worldwide recognize that digital security is a critical press freedom issue in the 21st century.

To protect journalists, their sources and their audiences, it is imperative that newsrooms use best-available security tools and practices, including encryption of sensitive communications and materials, anonymization of sources, and distribution of news through secure and censorship-resistant channels.

The organization's board of directors has included prominent journalists and whistleblowers such as Daniel Ellsberg, Laura Poitras, Glenn Greenwald, and Xeni Jardin, as well as activists, celebrities, and filmmakers. NSA whistleblower Edward Snowden joined FPF's board of directors in 2014 and began serving as its

President in early 2016.

The International Consortium of Investigative Journalists

Medical, Technological and Financial injustice are on the rise. The privacy and well-being of global citizens is under attack. The International Consortium of Investigative Journalists (ICIJ) is one of the few organizations stepping up to meet these challenges. ICIJ is an independent, Washington, D.C.-based international network of more than 200 investigative journalists and 100 media organizations in over 70 countries.

Launched in 1997 by the Center for Public Integrity, ICIJ was spun off in February 2017 into a fully independent organization working on issues of "cross-border crime, corruption, and the accountability of power." The ICIJ has exposed smuggling and tax evasion by multinational tobacco companies (2000), investigated organized crime syndicates, private military cartels, asbestos companies, and climate change lobbyists. ICIJ broke new ground by publicizing details of Iraq and Afghanistan war contracts.

Perhaps their biggest investigative success, The Panama Papers, was a collaboration of more than 100 media partners, including members of the Organized Crime and Corruption Reporting Project, with journalists who worked on the data, culminating in a partial release on 3 April 2016, which garnered global media attention.

The set of 11.5 million confidential financial and legal documents from the Panama-based law firm Mossack Fonseca included detailed information on more than

14,000 clients and more than 214,000 offshore entities, including the identities of shareholders and directors including noted personalities and heads of state—government officials and close relatives and associates of various heads of government of more than 40 other countries.

The German newspaper Süddeutsche Zeitung first received the released data from an anonymous source in 2015. After working on the Mossack Fonseca documents for a year, ICIJ director Gerard Ryle described how the offshore firm had "helped companies and individuals with tax havens, including those that have been sanctioned by the U.S. and UK."

In 2017, the ICIJ, the McClatchy Company, and the Miami Herald won the Pulitzer Prize for Explanatory

Reporting "for the Panama Papers, a series of stories using a collaboration of more than 300 reporters on six continents to expose the hidden infrastructure and global scale of offshore tax havens." In total, the ICIJ won more than 20 awards for the Panama Papers.

ICIJ is a unique organization. A U.S.-based nonprofit, it is both a small, resourceful newsroom with their own reporting team, as well as a global network of reporters and media organizations who work together to investigate the most important stories in the world. Their network of trusted members encompasses 267 of the best investigative reporters from 100 countries and territories. They also partner with more than 100 media organizations, from the world's most renowned outlets, including the BBC, the New York Times, the Guardian and the Asahi Shimbun, to small regional nonprofit investigative centers.

Drawing on the expertise and reach of their network, ICIJ collaborates on groundbreaking investigations that expose the truth and hold the powerful accountable, while also adhering to the highest standards of fairness and accuracy. The ICIJ core team is small, but ambitious. They empower their readers to engage with their local communities about issues of global importance, such as broken systems and abuses of power. They do that by harnessing the enormous strength of their extensive network.

In addition to their U.S. staff, they have team members in Australia, France, Spain, Hungary, Serbia, Belgium and Ireland. They are passionate about the power of journalism and provide the tools and guidance needed to successfully pull off unprecedented reporting collaborations. Over the years, ICIJ has released dozens of investigations—including the Pulitzer Prize-winning Panama Papers—and they have won many awards for their work. ICIJ is fully funded by donations. They encourage tips, leaks and story ideas from the public, whistleblowers, as well as from outstanding investigative journalists interested in collaborating with them.

The Million Hoodies Movement for Justice

When it comes to culture and modernity there are only a handful of organizations that can claim national and international success through a single and viral digital strategy. There is only one that has been recognized by the Pew Research Center for being the "first campaign in history to surpass a Presidential Election in terms of earned media." That's The Million Hoodies Movement for Justice.

Million Hoodies is a youth public policy and media justice organization founded in 2012 in the aftermath of the murder of Trayvon Martin, and continue to lead to this day.

In addition to pioneering a digital-first, cross-platform approach to Civil Rights organizing, Million Hoodies was one of earliest youth organizations to use text-based rapid mobilization with an organic message delivery model. With the help of our friends at NationBuilder, we also pioneered the use of leaderboards, tokens, micro-rewards and micro-mapping. The Virtual March On Washington was the first of its kind and we continue to have an impact on policy, reporting, Civil Rights and social justice. Our innovative approach to organizing has been recognized by some of the top media and philanthropic organizations in the world.

In 2013, Million Hoodies was the Grand Prize Winner of the Do Something Awards and received two Cannes Lions for Leadership and Innovation in Public Relations and Social Impact. Million Hoodies is a descendant of the Black Panther Party and the Million Man March. It is also the progenitor of the Movement for Black Lives (Black Lives Matter) and The Women's Movement. Our work continues the legacy of the Anti-Apartheid Movement through the use of music, media, art and entertainment to create historic social change.

We continue to leverage new technologies, platforms and approaches, including, but not limited to: Artificial

THEORY OF CHANGE

Intelligence (AI), User-generated content (UGC), Gaming, Geospatial Intelligence and a number of other innovative techniques and technologies.

We've been shot at, received death threats, survived deadly train accidents, trolling, biohacking, assassination and a myriad of other attacks and injustices. We've been slowed down, but nothing has stopped us. We continue to combat mass incarceration, criminalization, Islamophobia, the school-to-prison pipeline, fake news, targeting and trolling. Our media and policy work continues as well, both in the United States and abroad.

Our Theory of Change is simple: IF a small group of creative leaders and strategists come together to combat injustice, THEN effective, impactful and long-lasting change is possible. The precondition of our own safety and security has been taken from us over the years, but our work and impact continues.

9

THE EVOLUTION OF IMPACT

As the saying goes, there's more than one way to skin a cat. Given the size of the Global Impact Investing Market, $715 billion, there are many questions and concerns regarding the proper evaluation and evolution of Social Impact Programs and Theories of Change.

From Media & Entertainment to nonprofits, from charities to donors, and from multilateral and intergovernmental organizations to startups, there are a myriad of ways to measure, analyze, report, and improve Theories of Change and social impact programs. Our goal isn't to account for them all here, but rather to highlight the most successful, accurate and innovative ones. At the same time, it's important to remember that impact can be subjective and measurement can be inaccurate.

As we've seen, sometimes the best Theories of Change are expressed singularly, culturally and creatively. A dropped pot by Ai Weiwei. A Tribal dance around a flaming fire. A hoodie or hijab worn by millions. A lone figure facing off against a military tank. These are the images we remember; these are the moments that turn into movements.

THEORY OF CHANGE

When we prioritize practical impact, smart strategy, culture, creativity and expression over theory, indicators and interventions, we begin to see a new world of opportunities emerge, and glimpse the future of Theory of Change. Measurement and evaluation should flow naturally from this process, not interrupt or impede it.

One such forward thinking model is that developed and introduced by the Annie E. Casey Foundation. This model emphasizes *Impact*, *Influence* and *Leverage* as a means of measuring and evaluating change. I like this model because it addresses impact directly. It also acknowledges the influence of key players and assets who have significant leverage over various issues and causes.

This approach tends to make for a more accurate accounting of the qualitative and quantitative outcomes and indicators of a given social impact project or program. The addition of *leverage* and *influence* reflects changes in technology, media and governance, as well. This model gives the Annie E. Casey Foundation a more robust way to account for the impact of their funding and donation dollars.

When it comes to more traditional ways of measuring impact, there are, generally speaking, three or four different buckets that the data and indicators fall into: 1) **Actions**: Real world outcomes and actions taken; 2) **Items**: General items collected, signed or shared; 3) **Engagement (Online/Offline)**: Social Media impressions, engagement and sentiment; and 4) **Changes**: Number of laws changed, policies implemented and people or communities impacted. Every donor has their own preferences and procedures.

THEORY OF CHANGE

Ideally organizations are able to translate these numbers into real dollar amounts that can then be compared and contrasted to other organizations and shared with the rest of the world. The amount of earned media generated and dollars raised are obviously also important indicators and key performance factors collected by donors and organizations.

For founders and nonprofits, of course, the most important considerations are the actual outcomes themselves: 1) The Cost of Outcome Acquisition (COA)[4]; 2) The number of interventions needed to gain those outcomes; and 3) The growth or decline in the number, nature and size of the obstacles or issues

---

[4] Cost of Outcome Acquisition (COA) is the author's own term. It can be calculated both quantitatively and qualitatively, depending on the circumstances of the intervention. It is similar to Customer Acquisition Cost (CAC) or Lifetime Value (LTV) in Venture Capital.

themselves. These calculations can be simple and straightforward or quite convoluted and complex. In my experience, the more complicated they are the smaller the impact, and the less complicated they are, the bigger the impact. Again, simplicity, minimalism and accuracy are the name of the game when it comes to practical impact.

As a Digital Strategist with an expertise in Data Analytics, I've developed, evaluated and tested almost every indicator and approach out there, including a few of my own. It's hard to get it right and surprisingly easy to get it wrong. The number of donors, CEOs, founders and organizations who struggle with these calculations is actually much higher than you might expect.

If you find yourself falling into this bucket, don't worry, everyone has to start somewhere. There's always a helpful strategist or consultant like me just around the corner. And anyway, technology, social media, and social impact are evolving so quickly that as soon as you learn your way around, there will be a new system or methodology in place to replace the old one and take you in a completely new direction. Hopefully, after reading this book, you'll have a few ideas of your own on how to update and improve the world of social impact and social change.

Throughout my career, the most promising and impactful evaluation platforms and methods I've seen have been: Participant Media's Social Impact Index, The World Bank's Open Data Initiative, Hans Rosling's Gapminder Toolkit, Barry Wacksman's Functional Integration Framework, and the UN Sustainable Development Goals themselves (SDGs)—although the

SDGs are beginning to feel a bit on the slow side.

I believe the future of Theories of Change, especially with regard to modeling, measurement and evaluation, will come from one or more of these standout methodologies and platforms. Generally speaking, there will be a continued shift towards easier, increasingly innovative impact models and Theories of Change.

These will come from the industries and outfits adjacent to social change, including: Social Media, Marketing & Advertising, Business, Branding and Design, Technology and Innovation, and Startups and Venture Capital. As culture, trends and technology continue to converge, so too will ToCs and practical social impact continue to align. Artificial Intelligence, Automation, and Advanced Algorithms will also impact this space in ways that we can only begin to imagine. The very nature of AI and Automation is such that one day soon we will be able to go directly from obstacles presented to objectives reached with all indicators accounted for along the way. That day may have already arrived; at least it could be much closer than we think.

What implications and impact will these changes have on policy, society, charity, economics and education? Indeed, what impact will these changes have on society and the world itself? Is it possible to plan and envision the future of these sectors based on the new information at our disposal? If so, what impact will this have on ToCs themselves? Will we begin to go back to the future, so to speak? Or will the future begin to supplant the past completely?

It seems natural to me that ToCs will begin to look more and more like computer codes, AI Algorithms, and Machine Learning Models that can be tasked and trained to execute interventions to varying degrees of perfection. The execution of these algorithms will take place automatically across server networks, in-memory, and across Natural Language Processing Platforms (NLPs) like Lavalytics, Mordecai, and Liz.ai. That's just for starters.

Virtual Reality will no doubt add even more layers of information and impact that will take changemakers and charities in even more dynamic, immersive and engaging directions. Some of this is already happening, but, according to experts, the return on investment is not quite where it needs to be to be successful and sustainable in the long term. Perhaps a new company, donor, or nonprofit will come along soon and change all this. Maybe you.

10

THE FUTURE OF IMPACT

A Theory of change is a tool that can be used to improve or impede social impact. As we've seen, there is a difference between change management and practical impact. As we've also seen, there is math behind impact and Theory of Change, thus they can be improved mathematically.

ToCs are intended to help chart, measure and track social

change. The ToC methodology evolved out of the fields of Environmental and Organizational Psychology as a process for managing the objectives, impact and results of a given organization. As a guide to practical impact, ToCs tend to suffer from a handful of issues, including: Layers of dependency and bureaucracy; Linearity; Discontinuity; Cultural Limitations; Lack of Critical Theory; bad Pedagogy; and lack of Creativity, simplicity and Artistry.

That said, the Theory of Change model (or Change Management Model) introduced by Peter Drucker in 1954 continues to be a popular and useful way of managing change for charities, changemakers, movement builders and the like. It has been adapted, updated and transformed in many ways since its inception, most successfully, perhaps, by the Annie E. Casey Foundation with their emphasis on *Impact*, *Influence* and *Leverage*.

The most successful organizations place their Theory of Change into a macro "if, then" statement with high and low order goals, followed by a roadmap that typically includes their vision, mission, goals and program structure. This approach does seem to compliment strategic thinking and fundraising rather than frustrate it.

In my experience, Theories of Change must leave room for culture, critical theory, and new pedagogy in order to remain accurate, relevant and practical. In this way, a Theory of Change can be quite simple and straightforward, and social impact can be quite rapid and profound. A broken pot by Ai Weiwei. A Tribal dance beside a flaming fire. We can find examples of this cultural simplicity, ease and power everywhere we look and all throughout history, from the Anti-Apartheid Movement to the Movement for Black Lives.

We see it in works of art, poetry, literature, oratory, theater, cinema and TV. We feel it when we see it and we know it when we hear it. It is the combustion we see in chemical changes and the campfire around which we warm ourselves in the cold times of suffering and setback. It is far from just a theory, far from just an idea. In its purest form, it is the very basis of our humanity; the very thing that connects us to the future, to our destinies, and to one another.

The future of social impact is bright. The evolution of change management will begin to take place along increasingly algorithmic lines. The only obstacle in front of us is our own imagination.

THEORY OF CHANGE

Soon, those too will become automated, unburdened by the past and set free to continue changing and improving our world for the better.

Theory of Change can be simple. Social Impact can be immediate and profound. A Tribal dance around a flaming fire. A dropped pot by Ai Weiwei.

What will your Theory of Change be?

#MyToC

REFERENCES

1. "Cultural Relativism." Lumen, 26 Apr. 2021, courses.lumenlearning.com/culturalanthropology/chapter/cultural-relativism/.

2. Carter, Jacoby Adeshei, "Alain LeRoy Locke", The Stanford Encyclopedia of Philosophy (Summer 2012 Edition), Edward N. Zalta (ed.), URL = <https://plato.stanford.edu/archives/sum2012/entries/alain-locke/>.

3. Guy, Talmadge C. "ALAIN LOCKE." Adult Learning Unleashed Consulting, ALU Consulting, 26 Apr. 2021, www.alu-c.com/alain-locke.

4. The American International School of Johannesburg https://www.aisj-jhb.com/about-us

5. The International Baccalaureate Program (IB) https://www.ibo.org

6. The Hague Model United Nations (THIMUN) https://foundation.thimun.org

7. The American University (AU) https://www.american.edu

8. The Roosevelt Institute & Campus Network https://rooseveltinstitute.org

9. The Boys & Girls Clubs of America
   https://www.bgca.org

10. Southern Poverty Law Center (SPLC)
    https://www.splcenter.org

11. Freedom of the Press Foundation (FPF)
    https://freedom.press

12. International Consortium of Investigative Journalists (ICIJ) https://www.icij.org

13. Pew Research Center
    https://www.journalism.org/2012/03/30/special-report-how-blogs-twitter-and-mainstream-media-have-handled-trayvon-m/

14. https://www.instituteforpr.org/wp-content/uploads/PRR-Social-media-framing-within-the-Million-Hoodies-Movement-for-Justice.pdf

15. https://www.google.com/amp/s/www.denverpost.com/2013/09/06/daniel-maree-a-civil-rights-leader-for-the-21st-century/amp/

16. https://www.npr.org/sections/codeswitch/2013/07/24/205119191/after-zimmerman-verdict-activists-face-a-new-tougher-fight

17. https://www.thenation.com/article/archive/how-trayvon-martins-death-launched-new-generation-black-activism/tnamp/

THEORY OF CHANGE

ABOUT THE AUTHOR

Champion Muthle aka Daniel Maree is an award-winning Writer-Director, Creative and Cultural Strategist, Independent Journalist, Publisher, Civil Rights Leader, Inventor, Philosopher, Creative Technologist, Afro-Futurist, and Social Entrepreneur. He is a Frederick Douglass Scholar and Forbes 30 Under 30 Honoree for Social Entrepreneurship. His work has been featured in the MoMA and the Library of Congress.

www.ingramcontent.com/pod-product-compliance
Lightning Source LLC
Chambersburg PA
CBHW020437220526
45464CB00002B/740